Josh and the Thunder

Written by Simon Mugford

Illustrated by Gabby Grant

Collins

It felt too hot in the garden.

3

Just then, the children felt some rain land on them.

As the children sat down for lunch, the thunder erupted.

Josh did not like the crash of the thunder.

There was a flash of light.

Josh did a jump at the flash.
He did not like it.

Josh felt sad.

11

Emma had a torch and a drum
in her tent.

13

Thunder and rain

After reading

Letters and Sounds: Phase 4

Word count: 99

Focus on adjacent consonants with short vowel phonemes, e.g. c/r/a/sh

Common exception words: of, the, I, he, we, me, was, like, some, come, there

Curriculum links (EYFS): Understanding the World: The World

Curriculum links (National Curriculum, Year 1): Geography

Early learning goals: Understanding: answer "how" and "why" questions about their experiences and in response to stories or events; Reading: children use phonic knowledge to decode regular words and read them aloud accurately, read some common irregular words

National Curriculum learning objectives: Spoken language: listen and respond appropriately to adults and their peers; Reading/word reading: read aloud accurately books that are consistent with their developing phonic knowledge and that do not require them to use other strategies to work out words; Reading/comprehension: develop pleasure in reading, motivation to read, vocabulary and understanding by making inferences on the basis of what is being said and done

Developing fluency

- Your child may enjoy hearing you read the book.
- Look at pages 10 to 11 together. Model reading the main text on page 10. Then read the speech bubble on page 11 with lots of expression. Draw attention to the exclamation mark and talk about how we might read sentences with an exclamation mark with more expression and enthusiasm.
- Now look at pages 12 to 13. Ask your child if they can see any exclamation marks. Read the main text on page 12 and ask your child to read the speech bubbles with expression.

Phonic practice

- Practise reading words that contain adjacent consonants. Model sound talking the following word, saying each of the sounds quickly and clearly. Then blend the sounds together, e.g. f/e/l/t
- Ask your child to sound talk and blend the words **crash**, **flash** and **thunder**.

Extending vocabulary

- Look at pages 6 to 8. Talk about the words in capital letters that are used to describe the thunder and lightning: **crash**, **bang**, **flash**.